BLAKE HAS THE BLUES

By BLAKE HOENA

Illustrated by LUKE FLOWERS

Music Arranged and Produced by MARK OBLINGER

CANTATA
LEARNING

WWW.CANTATALEARNING.COM

CANTATA
LEARNING

Published by Cantata Learning
1710 Roe Crest Drive
North Mankato, MN 56003
www.cantatalearning.com

A note to educators and librarians from the publisher: Cantata Learning has provided the following data to assist in book processing and suggested use of Cantata Learning product.

Publisher's Cataloging-in-Publication Data
Prepared by Librarian Consultant: Ann-Marie Begnaud
Library of Congress Control Number: 2015958179
    Blake Has the Blues
    Series: Read, Sing, Learn : Sound It Out!
    By Blake Hoena
    Illustrated by Luke Flowers
    Summary: A song about the bl letter blend.
    ISBN: 978-1-63290-610-6 (library binding/CD)
    ISBN: 978-1-63290-560-4 (paperback/CD)
Suggested Dewey and Subject Headings:
    Dewey: E FIC
    LCSH Subject Headings: Emotions – Juvenile humor. | Emotions – Songs and music – Texts. | Emotions – Juvenile sound recordings.
    Sears Subject Headings: Emotions – Humor. | Phonetics. | School songbooks. | Children's songs. | Jazz music.
    BISAC Subject Headings: JUVENILE FICTION / Social Themes / Emotions & Feelings. | JUVENILE FICTION / Stories in Verse. | JUVENILE FICTION / Humorous Stories.

Book design and art direction, Tim Palin Creative
Editorial direction, Flat Sole Studio
Music direction, Elizabeth Draper
Music arranged and produced by Mark Oblinger

Printed in the United States of America in North Mankato, Minnesota.
072016   0335CGF16

ACCESS THE MUSIC!

SCAN CODE WITH MOBILE APP

CANTATALEARNING.COM

Take the letter B. Now add an L. Put them together to make the BL sound. This sound lets you *bl*ink your eyes, *bl*ow a horn, and *bl*ush when you feel shy. Usually, you will find the BL sound at the beginning of a word.

The BL sound sure is handy when you have the *bl*ues. Now turn the page and sing along!

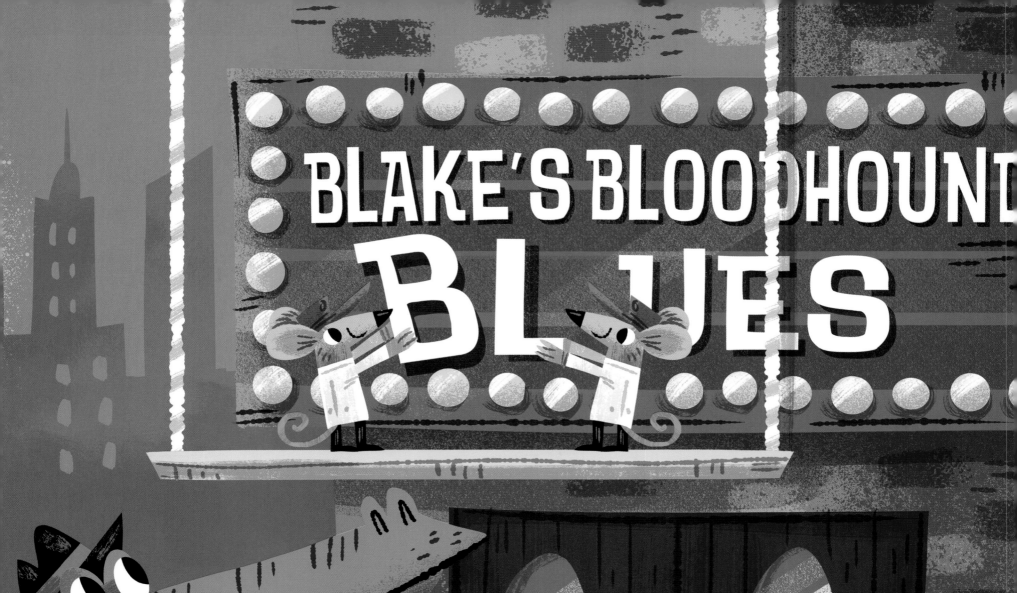

Blake has the blues.
Oh, Blake has the blues.
He has the blubbering **bloodhound** blues.

Blake has the blues.

Oh, Blake has the blues.

The blubbering blues have him howling this tune.

Arooooooooo!

Late last night, we had a snowy **blizzard**.
Blake was outside in the **blustery** wind.
He slipped on some ice and—blam!

8

Blake's blues guitar was blown away,
and he was sent for a spin.

Blake has the blues.

Oh, Blake has the blues.

He has the blubbering bloodhound blues.

Blake has the blues.

Oh, Blake has the blues.

The blubbering blues have him howling this tune.

Aroooooooooo!

Early this morning, Blake tossed off his blanket, and in the pitch black, he jumped out of bed. Blake took just two steps and—blam!

Blake tripped on some wooden blocks
and got a blue bump on his head!

Blake has the blues.

Oh, Blake has the blues.

He has the blubbering bloodhound blues.

Blake has the blues.

Oh, Blake has the blues.

The blubbering blues have him howling this tune.

Aroooooooooo!

WORLDS BEST DOG

BLAKE

Listen to Blake howl
Ar-arooooooooo,

while Blaine the blue jay
blows on her **blues harp,**

and Blair the blue whale sings,
"Bleep blop, a blip blap bloo.

Bleepity bloopity.
Bleep blop, a blip blap bloo."

17

The next day, Blake saw a flower blossom.
The bloodhound gave the **bluebell** a sniff.
Then he started to sneeze and—blam!

In the blink of an eye,
Blake was blown off a cliff.

Blake blushed as he waved bye-bye!

Blake has the blues.

Oh, Blake has the blues.

He has the blubbering bloodhound blues.

Blake has the blues.

Oh, Blake has the blues.

The blubbering blues have him howling this tune.

Aroooooooooo!

SONG LYRICS
Blake Has the Blues

Blake has the blues.
Oh, Blake has the blues.
He has the blubbering
  bloodhound blues.

Blake has the blues.
Oh, Blake has the blues.
The blubbering blues have him
  howling this tune.
Arooooooooo!

Late last night, we had a
  snowy blizzard.
Blake was outside in the blustery wind.
He slipped on some ice and—blam!

Blake's blues guitar was blown away,
and he was sent for a spin.

Blake has the blues.
Oh, Blake has the blues.
He has the blubbering
  bloodhound blues.

Blake has the blues.
Oh, Blake has the blues.
The blubbering blues have him
  howling this tune.
Arooooooooo!

Early this morning, Blake tossed
  off his blanket,
and in the pitch black, he jumped out
  of bed.
Blake took just two steps and—blam!

Blake tripped on some wooden blocks
and got a blue bump on his head!

Blake has the blues.
Oh, Blake has the blues.
He has the blubbering
  bloodhound blues.

Blake has the blues.
Oh, Blake has the blues.
The blubbering blues have him
  howling this tune.
Arooooooooo!

Listen to Blake howl
Ar-arooooooooo,

while Blaine the blue jay
blows on her blues harp,

and Blair the blue whale sings,
"Bleep blop, a blip blap bloo.
Bleepity bloppy.
Bleep blop, a blip blap bloo."

The next day, Blake saw a
  flower blossom.
The bloodhound gave the bluebell
  a sniff.
Then he started to sneeze and—blam!

In the blink of an eye,
Blake was blown off a cliff.

Blake blushed as he waved bye-bye!

Blake has the blues.
Oh, Blake has the blues.
He has the blubbering
  bloodhound blues.

Blake has the blues.
Oh, Blake has the blues.
The blubbering blues have him
  howling this tune.
Arooooooooo!

Blake Has the Blues

Blues
Mark Oblinger

Chorus

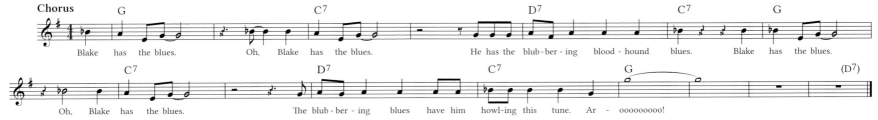

Blake has the blues. Oh, Blake has the blues. He has the blub-ber-ing blood-hound blues. Blake has the blues.

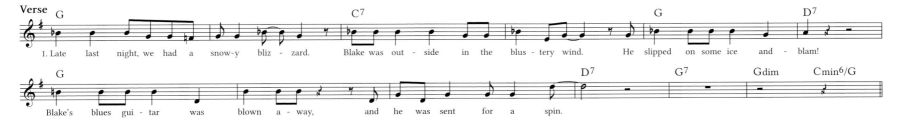

Oh, Blake has the blues. The blub-ber-ing blues have him howl-ing this tune. Ar - ooooooooo!

Verse

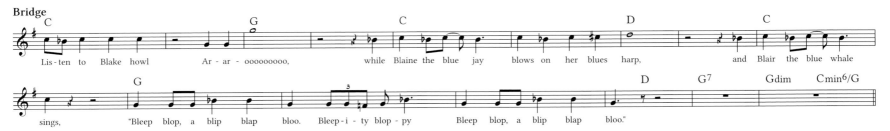

1. Late last night, we had a snow-y bliz-zard. Blake was out - side in the blus-tery wind. He slipped on some ice and—blam!

Blake's blues gui-tar was blown a-way, and he was sent for a spin.

Chorus

Verse 2
Early this morning, Blake tossed off his blanket,
and in the pitch black, he jumped out of bed.
Blake took just two steps and—blam!
Blake tripped on some wooden blocks
and got a blue bump on his head!

Chorus

Bridge

Lis-ten to Blake howl Ar - ar - ooooooooo, while Blaine the blue jay blows on her blues harp, and Blair the blue whale

sings, "Bleep blop, a blip blap bloo. Bleep-i-ty blop-py Bleep blop, a blip blap bloo."

Verse 3
The next day, Blake saw a flower blossom.
The bloodhound gave the bluebell a sniff.
Then he started to sneeze and—blam!
In the blink of an eye,
Blake was blown off a cliff.
Blake blushed as he waved bye-bye!

Chorus

GLOSSARY

blizzard—a snowstorm with very strong winds

bloodhound—a kind of dog with a long face and big floppy ears; bloodhounds have an excellent sense of smell

blubbering—crying

bluebell—a plant with lots of small blue flowers that look like little bells

blues harp—a harmonica

blustery—very windy

GUIDED READING ACTIVITIES

1. Imagine a creature who can only say BL words, such as blap or bloo. Give the animal a BL name. Make up a fake language for your pet. It's okay if it does not make sense!

2. Blues is a type of jazz music. Some famous blues singers were B.B. King and Billie Holiday. With an adult's help, go online and listen to a blues song by one of these artists. Did you like the song?

TO LEARN MORE

Gaiman, Neil. *Blueberry Girl*. New York: HarperCollins, 2011.

Novesky, Amy. *Mister and Lady Day: Billie Holiday and the Dog Who Loved Her*. New York: Harcourt, 2013.

Rissman, Rebecca. *Blue*. Mankato, MN: Heinemann-Raintree, 2012.

Troupe, Thomas Kingsley. *Blow It Up!* Mankato, MN: Capstone Press, 2013.